IT'S NOT OK.
AND THAT'S OK.

BENJAMIN J. HARTINGS

Copyright © 2016 Benjamin J. Hartings

All rights reserved.

ISBN: 0-9862179-1-3
ISBN-13: 978-0-9862179-1-3

DEDICATION

To those who cared for us…as we endured for Him.

With Love,

Benjamin & Lynn Hartings

CONTENTS

Acknowledgments   i

Preface   ii

1. It's ok to Grieve.   Pg 1
   It's not ok to Lose Hope.

2. It's ok to Stop.   Pg 23
   It's not ok to Quit.

3. It's ok to Relish the Sunrise.   Pg 46
   It's not ok to Hide from the Sunset.

4. It's ok to be Angry.   Pg 64
   It's not ok to be Bitter.

5. It's ok to have Fear.   Pg 96
   It's not ok to be Afraid.

It's Not Ok. And That's Ok.

ACKNOWLEDGMENTS

To our family who loved us.
Our friends who cared for us.
And our doctors who cured us.

To those who share their stories with us, so we can share their lessons with you. From near to far, each one of you have impacted first the joy in our lives, and a distant second, the writing of this book. Your inspiration in our hearts has turned into the words in this book.

To those who supported us in this writing, in word and in prayer.

Andy, Phil, Kevin, Matt, Julie, Joyce, Dianne, Chris, Jim, Ryan, Joe, Conor, Adam, Rachel, Rebecca, Meredith, Conor, Chad, Conor, Jeff, Amy, Matt, Marc, Kristy, Ed, Jessica, Lisa, Erin, Fr. Tom, Dave, Ginny, Jim, Patrick, Dan, Aaron and so many others that may hereto go unnamed.

To those who have supported my mission, who listen to my rambling, non-sensical wondering spirit and who point me forever upward for direction.

And for the small band of editors, you know who you are. This book would not exist if not for you.

Throughout the book, references to Christian Biblical Scripture are made. When referencing this Scripture, this book uses a few specific translations. For your benefit, they are footnoted in the text and listed here. I would encourage you to reference the Scripture as you read.

NIV
New International Version

GNT
Good News Translation

ESV
English Standard Version

NABRE
New American Bible Revised Edition

NLT
New Living Translation

BENJAMIN J. HARTINGS

PREFACE

From time to time I will randomly search for a hashtag on Facebook just to see what pops up. One day, I searched for the hashtag *#Blessed*. The tweets there were so joy-filled and happy.

Married yesterday! #Blessed

Got a new Job! #Blessed

Admitted to my dream school! #Blessed

So peaceful and relaxing this morning! #Blessed

Eight years ago the man of my dreams asked me to marry him…so #Blessed!

Offered a Scholarship #Blessed

One young man had a post that included all of these hashtags…

#Blessed #Loved #Smiles #Joy #Worshiping #God #Praying #Dating #Jesus

It was awesome to see his smiling face with his girlfriend at a winter conference worshiping God!

But then I paused…and asked the question,

"What if Jesus was on Facebook?."

"What if when I typed in @*Jesus*, I found the man of the Gospels?"

Perhaps his hashtags would look like this…

#Blessed to be poor in spirit today!

#Blessed today as I mourn!

#Blessed am I who is being made meek and humble of heart by my enemies!

#Blessed to be thirsting for righteousness!

#Blessed to be forgiving those who hate me today!

#Blessed to risk my life to be a peacemaker!

#Blessed to be persecuted!

#Blessed to be enduring this trial!

Makes you pause, doesn't it.

In 2013, I stood with my wife on the second story of a suburban house in Columbus, Ohio. Our child was dead. Dreams were shattered like broken glass on the floor. We buried him only weeks before this day as we held each other in a tear-filled embrace.

Our tears were mixed in sadness, grief, worry and pain. Grief from our son had just begun to heal in our hearts when a freight train came barreling through the foundation of our lives.

On that chilly October day, we had received the news that I had cancer…and not just one form, but two unique forms of cancer.

My son was gone. And now, I'm at death's doorstep. At only thirty three years old, we were living a nightmare.

Going into 2013, we were young, virulent and healthy. We were fit, formed and faithful. My wife Lynn was pregnant with our fourth child, I was embarking on a career change and we had dreams in our eyes.

Eleven months later, in early December 2013, I now stood trembling - literally, every single bone of my body was physically shaking - trying to shoulder the weight of the news that not only had my son died, but now I stood on the brink of death…

THIS IS NOT OK!!!!

I had screamed these words at the top of my lungs upon the death of my son months before. But now I was so tired and weak from surgery, I could not lash out.

I could only mutter those words under my breath between the sobbing and tears that were wetting Lynn's head as we embraced.

THIS IS NOT OK GOD!!!!

Amidst that crisis, for the first time in my life, I felt the warmth of an embrace only a splintered spirit and broken body can feel - *I felt the hands of God wrap us in a holy embrace picking our body and spirit on high.* And I heard the words that I will never forget, spoken directly into my heart.

> *Yes, I know it's not OK.*
> *Ben, but that's OK.*

God spoke to me.

He spoke to me in an audible voice so clear and distinct that as I write this, I can still hear his words.

He said, *Yes this is not OK. You have cancer. But trust me. Trust me!*

And in that embrace, a flood of love covered us sealing our hearts instantly from oppression and anxiety. Immediately we knew deep in our spirit that regardless of the outcome, it would be OK.

This embrace of God was divine, spirit quenching, soul satisfying rest - like that which I've never felt before. The words shared at that moment were eternal and unending.

It was not OK. But that was OK.

Because HE, God, had us in his arms.

For the first time ever, I felt the embrace of God.

God had previously walked *with us* through our lives. But like the Footsteps poem we know so well, now He began to *carry* us. And the storm was so violent, we had no other choice but to trust in Him.

As I write this, I am reminded of a quote by Fr. Richard Rohr.

> *We cannot attain the presence of God because we're already totally in the presence of God. What is absent is the awareness.*
> Fr. Richard Rohr, What the Mystics Know

I believe we had always been in God's presence. Married in a Catholic Church, washed in the waters of baptism and flooded with the power of the Holy Spirit. But I was not aware of it, because I did not <u>need</u> God.

I am a child of God and unless I acknowledge I need him, like my own living children need me, they will not know I am there. They ask for dinner, help with homework and counsel on friendships. They acknowledge me and need my help.

While God was there in my life, I was not aware of his presence. He sat quietly in the living room of my life while I ran from fire to fire all the while waiting for me to cry out to Him.

Jesus hash-tags #Blessed on his Facebook page with posts that I did not understand before that day in my upper room. In our upper room, a shield of protection covered us in the armor of God. It was a moment of clarity. Jesus' Gospel is preached from truth, acknowledging and encouraging us to embrace the circumstances of our lives for *His* glory.

It's the reason why we write this book.

What changed us about that year?

Life changed.
Love changed.
Relationships changed.
Our children changed.
Priorities changed.

I changed. Lynn changed.
We changed.

For the first time in our lives, we had the props totally knocked out from underneath us. We had no safety net below and we were free falling into the abyss…and that's when God stepped in.

Now, I can help you my son.

Like Superman on a mission from heaven, He caught us in mid-air lifted our spirits high and fixed our eyes unto the horizon.

That afternoon did not cure me from cancer. It did not heal my grief stricken heart. But it welled up a spirit in us that continues to overflow with Joy unto this day.

God had empathy for our situation. And all He asked for was our faith.

Weeks later has this armor began to solidify, my wife and I recalled Proverbs 4: 25-26 (ESV) where God instructed us to:

> *"Let your eyes look directly ahead and let your gaze be fixed straight in front of you. Watch the path of your feet And all your ways will be established."*

The circumstances of losing our son James and then immediately facing life-threatening illness as left us nothing but God in whom to trust. Everything changed from that moment forward. God was not only with us, but he carried us.

> We were fearful, but not afraid.
> We were full of grief, but had not lost hope.
>
> We were young, still in the sunrise of life,
> But we were not going to look past the sunset.

> We needed to stop to collect ourselves,
> But we were not going to quit.

It was not OK. And that was OK.

We trusted in him and let his will be done. For it was not our will, but His.

> "For My thoughts are not your thoughts. Nor are your ways My ways," declares the LORD. "For as the heavens are higher than the earth, so are My ways higher than your ways and My thoughts than your thoughts."
> Isaiah 55:8-9 ESV

His thoughts were greater than our thoughts. My anxiety turned to worship.

His ways are higher than my ways. My pain turned to prayer for my wife and children.

God's pathway for our lives has been a fountain of Joy!

God's grace covered the rest of our journey and weeks after recovering from surgery, I stood at the front door of the James Cancer Hospital knowing chemotherapy would begin the moment I walked through the door. I couldn't do it.

In the anxiety, I prayed, and He carried me in.

When I could not sleep and cried in the lost memories with my son. He held me in his arms.

In the middle of treatment, when the pain became too much, so much so I was ready to die…He heard my cry and in restful waters bathed me in peace.

He was there!
He is here!

It was not OK. But in His presence, it was OK!

I am truly #Blessed!

This journey inspired us to write this book. It is inspired by our experience.

Our journey in 2013 was divine and through a crack in heaven's gate created by sickness & mourning in our lives - we were overcome by a flood of God's faithfulness and grace.

Our story, from February 2013 to July 2014 with so much pain in the span of a year, was shared with many. The death of our son James was enough for a lifetime. But God had more, and cancer attacked and singled me out. We had so many people covering us in prayer. And in the years since, we have had so many people reach out to us for help. Our story is the same every time. God's plan not ours. Go to your upper room and give it God, be in His shower of grace. allowing Him to clean you of fear, anger, pain and heartache.

And as we heard their stories, it was the same as ours. God's faithfulness prevailed, and his love never ended. The armor of God protected their heart, spirit and Joy permeated and overflowed in abundance.

From our own experience and those we have counseled in the years since, we know that life is not OK. But, ultimately it was OK because of Jesus. At the cross, his blood ran red and sin, death, pain and grief were washed white, cleaned from the garments of life.

Through it all, He had set and renewed our anchor firmly in the veil.

> *This hope is a strong and trustworthy anchor for our souls. It leads us through the curtain into God's inner sanctuary.*
> *Hebrews 6: 19 ESV*

We wrote this book based on the events of our lives. It is personal but also communal. There is a community of those close to us who walked with us and with whom we now walk in this journey.

Sharing moments in life when life was not OK forged in steel a bond of love. Specific moments, like when a loved one dies, when cancer diagnosis comes or when a debilitating illness steals the one we love are shared.

The journey of life is imperfect. But I'm reminded of a quote from C.S. Lewis.

> *Hardships often prepare ordinary people for an extraordinary destiny.*

Faith in Christ reveals the extraordinary in each of us. His destiny is accomplished through our life.

Life will not be perfect. But He is.

May the Peace of Christ be with you always. And may his peace dwell in you as you discover that in Him, it's OK no matter the circumstances of this life.

~ Benjamin & Lynn Hartings
   December 4, 2016

The Lord is at hand; do not be anxious about anything, but in everything by prayer and supplication with thanksgiving let your requests be made known to God. And the peace of God, which surpasses all understanding, will guard your hearts and your minds in Christ Jesus.

Philippians 4: 6-7

NIV

CHAPTER 1

It's ok to Grieve.
It's _not_ ok to Lose Hope.

The capacity to grieve equals that of our love.
The greater we love, the greater our grief will be.
Therefore, the deeper we grieve, the more we loved.
Then, embrace our grief as an honor to the loved one lost.
~Benjamin Hartings~

Conor was a great athlete. He played college basketball earning numerous awards, winning a national championship and being named an All-American. Conor was raised by what I would call a "strong" father. I perceive strong fathers to be those that are invested - in time, talent and treasure - for the future of their children.

Conor's father Dave was an invested Dad. He had three children. Early in his life he decided that teaching his children the ethics of strong work, love and sacrifice would be part of his legacy. He worked multiple jobs to provide for his family, as a teacher, painter and handyman. With the money he made, he traversed the path of private Christian school, college and pioneered his children into adulthood.

I had a chance to be with Dave and Conor often. Conor happened to be my age, a man of faith and an invested father to his own children. As neighbors, Conor and I quickly developed a friendship. We shared a heritage of college athletics, a mission to raise our family and a bond as brothers in Jesus Christ. Conor became a growing oak tree in my life under whose shade I could find rest.

As the years went by, I met Conor's father Dave at neighborhood gatherings. I learned his father had kept his painting business into the early years of his retirement so when my home needed a refresh - we of course went to Dave for help. In this need, Dave spent time at our home. He spent hours painting, talking with my wife and children. During those days, I learned where Conor's foundation of grace originated, in the deep love of his father for Jesus. I understood where his son and my neighbor received such love, dedication and life. Dave had invested all he had - all his time, talent and treasure - into the rearing of his family.

During that same period of life, I was exposed to Dr. James Dobson, a world renowned speaker, writer and teacher on the family. Dr. Dobson founded the ministry Focus on the Family. Dr. Dobson was not my neighbor, but I had a chance to meet his son Ryan Dobson at a crisis pregnancy care center event on a cool fall evening. As I learned the story of Ryan's adoption by Dr. Dobson and his wife, a theme carried through from Dave to Dr. Dobson's.

Dr. Dobson was a strong, invested father to his son Ryan. He had invested time, talent and treasure into Ryan. At one point early on in his career and his marriage, Dr. Dobson actually sold one of his cars, taking their family from two cars in the driveway to simply one, in order to "finance" the opportunity for his wife to stay at home. They literally "ate" the proceeds from the sale of the Volkswagen while his wife stayed at home with their children and Dr. Dobson completed his educational studies. He put his money where his mouth is and invested his treasure in the future of his children.

Dr. Dobson's knowledge of this kind of sacrificial love ran deep. He inherited it from generations past. His grandfather, a traveling preacher, had early success in his life, only to give it up for his children. His grandfather was "on the circuit", preaching nationwide. His name became known due to his willingness and ability to preach the Gospel. This call on his heart to preach was only inferior to his call to parent his children and love his wife.

And when the time came, he sacrificed his pathway forward to worldly recognition, to be recognized as the father of his home. He invested his time in children, rather than worldwide evangelical preaching.

Those figures of manhood are not isolated. Many, many women of grace have carried the same call.

I am reminded of a young mother with whom my children attended school. She was a mother of two young children and a wife to a successful, loving husband. Her name was Mary Ann. Mary Ann had married the man of her dreams and found grace in her vocation to her children.

Then at age 32, she was diagnosed with cancer and the calm waters of the sea turned to a raging storm. She was put through misery with surgery, chemotherapy, reconstruction, infection, re-occurrence and fresh new battles every day. Along the way, she did not press inward in her focus, worried only about herself. But rather she focused upon the loved ones in her life.

She continued to be a wife to a loving husband and a mother to young children. Mary Ann fought like the battle was to win. She measured victories not in health - but in life. She loved deeply, shared freely and had faith the Lord would provide means for her family to prosper.

Neighbors, school networks and church communities all stepped up to raise support, with time for their children while they traveled for appointments, treasure to support the endeavors of medical care and talent to help consult for any desired needs around the house. The love in the house and in the community for her family only grew with time.

The same community had grown around Dave and Conor, but by different circumstances. As more people were impacted by the talents of Dave's life: His dedication to quality craftsmanship as a painter. His truth teaching at a Christian school. And his faithfulness as a steward of his money - more people came to love Dave.

I came to love the stories he shared. And was changed by his role as a father and husband.

Then tragically, Dave died suddenly of a massive heart attack on a job site at age 64. He lived a life of so much love and compassion that his funeral was attended by nearly 500 people. Each one had been impacted by him and his family. So many people were grieved and to this very day, the loss of Dave is painful for the family.

Mary Ann's story tragically ended the same way. Despite her faithful spirit, her physical fight with cancer ended at age of 34. She was an amazing mother. Mary Ann showed the depth and breadth of love for another in the care she had for her family - especially as a wife to her husband Dominic all the way to the end of life. I know her husband. He has begun to date again, but only after a long-suffering heart skipped many beats.

While Dave and Mary Ann both passed away way too young, Dr. Dobson's grandfather did not die suddenly, or at a young age. Dobson writes of the life and loss of his Grandfather in his book, "Bringing up Boys," speaking about what it is like to live a life full of love.

His grandfather, R.L. Dobson, died surrounded by all his family. Upon drawing his last breath, there was weeping and mourning - a loss that was deeply felt by all who loved him.

Grief

Dave, Mary Ann and R.L. Dobson met the end with faith, hope and an enduring love that left behind families in a tidal wave of grief. It is the natural order - birth, life and death.

Death marks the end of a short journey on earth. During this journey, seeds are planted by men and women in our lives. As they sprout and grow, we can't see living without the shade of the trees.

But upon death, those trees are ripped out of our lives. An oak tree fallen, now we can only watch the leaves wither away. Sometimes slowly as in the death of R.L. Dobson. And sometimes quickly, as in the death of Dave or MaryAnn.

As these trees are torn from our lives, a deep inconsolable cloud of grief replaces the shade of the the deeply rooted tree.

I experienced this deep grief when my son James passed away from this life. His cycle, from birth, life and death was short, but meaningful beyond words. He lived only 90 minutes outside the womb, dying of a birth defect that shut down his internal organs only minutes after birth. He was perfect in appearance, but contained fatally-flawed organs which limited his breadth of life.

My love for James is not measured in hours, days or weeks, but is deeply rooted in the words "Father" and "Mother."

When our son died, for the first time in my life I experienced the cloud of grief. I sunk inward and found in the recesses of my heart places I did not know existed. This grief scared me, exposing spaces hidden in the dark for decades or more.

And what I knew about myself changed. Places inside me once flush with flowers, I now found replaced by the parched, barren landscape of grief.

When I lost James, I seemed to fall deeper into despair. In the weeks and months after his death, I began to wonder if I'd ever get out of the fog that consumed my life. When I thought I reached bottom, the floor would once again fall out from underneath me. New expanses of grief would be found and tears would flow again, and again, and again.

While I was searching for the bottom, what I discovered was the depths of my own heart...and in those depths I found an unexpected answer. What I was discovering was not death and grief, but it was the *depth of my love for James*.

When Conor's father Dave passed away suddenly, he shared the same experience with me. Conor told me the depth of love for his father was unknown until he died. And when he died, it was such a deep, deep loss it was almost incomprehensible.

Conor shared that upon hearing the news of his father's death at a local bar/restaurant, he literally lost control, falling to his knees overcome by grief. Sobbing ensued for not moments but days and weeks. The loss overcame his spirit because the death of his father was so intense.

What Conor and I had discovered was the same thing the families of R.L. Dobson and Mary Ann had discovered. That in death, the love of the lost is exposed, often for the first time to the full light of day. And as the depth of your love had grown through life, in increments of time and experience together, so too the increments of grief will expand over our capacity to endure it.

And yes, we may break.

Tears will flow. Sobbing may overcome us. The inability to rise out of bed may force us to stop.

But this is what I learned in these moments. I learned that in the death of my son…

> ***The capacity to grieve expands in direct correlation to the depth of our Love.***
>
> ***Therefore, the deeper we love…The deeper our grief will be when your loved one is lost.***

Grief is a feeling of deep sorrow caused by the death of a loved one. That sorrow can manifest itself in so many ways. Anger, despair, dejection, emotion, tears, heartache, anguish and pain are only a few words of description.

When my son died, my grief carried every single one of those words and many more. Three years after his death, I still harbor tears, emotion, heartache and anger over the loss. The "what if's", reminders and growth of my other children provide constant reminders of this loss.

My son Thomas wrote a simple book at school for his teacher in first grade two years after James' death. He spoke about his favorite sport, laminated it and brought it home. The last page was an about the author page, where he wrote...

"I have two sisters and <u>two</u> brothers."

Yes he has two brothers, but only one of them living...*Insert knife and twist once again*...My grief is at a depth and breadth incomprehensibly large - and it's size is still being discovered daily.

I however do not believe that grief is a disease to be cured through a five step process. I don't believe it is something we should "get over" or "move on" from.

I believe that grief is rather a physical separation. That we grieve something physically lost in this life. I believe that grief exposes something beautiful - the love for the person who is now gone.

Let's be clear here.

The death of a loved one *is not Ok*.

It is not meant to be a fun-filled experience when we physically separate in death from our loved ones.

Death is hard.

Death is permanent.

But, death is also life.

The word death itself is often not mentioned when we speak to others grieving. We may rather say our loved one "passed on," "passed away" or "we lost our loved one." Saying "death or dying" in reference to our loved one brings with it a weight.

While this weight is heavy. It is not meant to drag us down. This weight represents an eternal weight of a glory beyond compare.

And while death is not ok, it was not a part of God's original plan...I do believe this weight of grief is ok.

It is Ok to Grieve.

I believe grief is honorable, truth filled, spirit-lifting and ordained as an ordered reality to create longing for our eternal home with Christ. This weight we experience is meant to turn us toward the one who can carry the weight for us.

Grief is Deep in Scripture

The tradition of wearing sack cloths and sitting in ashes in the Old Testament is meant to show this longing. At Jewish funerals, the family commits to sit *Shiva*, which means sitting on a wooden stool or a low wooden box for seven days after a loved one's death. By this symbol, they show that mourning and grief does not just take over part of your body - it takes over your whole body... and also your mind, heart and soul.

Wearing of sackcloth and ashes and sitting on a hard wooden stool is a symbolic gesture of pain and sorrow for the death of a loved one.

When R.L. Dobson passed and Mary Ann succumb to cancer there were no sack cloths present at the funeral. When Dave died of a heart attack and James was buried, ashes were not present at the funeral services. However, inside everyone was a feeling of vacancy. We grieved this void as a family as Jesus had done in the death of Lazarus. In John's Gospel this account is shared.

> *"Where have you laid him (Lazarus)?" he asked.*
> *"Come and see, Lord," they replied.*
> *Jesus wept.*
> *Then the Jews said, "See how he <u>loved</u> him!"*
> ~ John 11: 34-36 NIV

Jesus hurt. He was not sheltered from grief. Despite the fact he was about to raise him back to life, he sobbed with the family.

But Jesus also knew this was temporary. He lifted his eyes to heaven and wept because of the grief experienced by his family and friends. He hurt for them.

So I recall when my body hurts, my mind is overwhelmed and my spirits aches…that Jesus aches for me.

But as in the Old New Testament tradition of "sackcloth and ashes," where this wooly, itchy cloth was worn for a time and then removed; we too are called to look forward. The Jewish tradition of sitting Shiva was not a permanent change to life. Rather after seven days, there is a gathering of friends and family to honor the dead and burn the stool which was part of the grieving process.

This may seem quick. To me it is very quick. But remember, the removing of the stool is only symbolic. At my son's death I actually made a stool and put his footprints on it. I have not burnt, thrown away or discarded this treasure of mine. My son's stool is with me daily.

His wooden stool will be with me as long as I'm here on earth. I remember him when I am eating, working, worshiping and celebrating with family and friends. His short stool sits in my bathroom, at my feet every morning and every night.

The tradition is for the sackcloth to be worn as a prayer for forgiveness & repentance. It was also worn as a prayer for deliverance from the sorrow and for the day we too will die. This prayer is not made out of fear, anger, sorrow or anguish. It is made with one with a focus on *Hope*!

John Piper in his Book titled, *"Don't Waste your Cancer"* has a chapter titled, *"We waste our cancer if we grieve as those who have no hope"* which states this:

Paul used this phrase about grieving without hope in relation to those whose loved ones had died:

"We do not want you to be uninformed, brothers, about those who are asleep, that you may not grieve as others do who have no hope" (1 Thessalonians 4:13 ESV).

There is a grief at death. Even for the believer who dies, there is temporary loss—loss of body, and loss of loved ones here, and loss of earthly ministry. But the grief is different—it is permeated with hope.

"We would rather be away from the body and at home with the Lord" (2 Corinthians 5:8 ESV). Don't waste your cancer grieving as those who don't have this hope.

The hope of which Mr. Piper speaks is what permeates and overcomes my grief. Just as Jesus permeates and overcomes the grave.

Jesus himself was grieved upon the death of Lazarus. And again filled with grief upon his own death. Reading Luke 22, which has the account of Jesus' final moments in the Garden of Gethsemane once more, I discovered Jesus was physically, emotionally and spiritually exhausted – he could have slept – just like his disciples were sleeping. He probably wanted to sleep, but he knew the trials ahead would need the allegiance of his Father. So instead he stayed with God on that night. He knelt in prayer, with his human life on the line.

He faced temptation.

He faced fear.

He asked for his father's allegiance.

And yet Jesus endured. Wanting to sleep. But not sleeping. Not because he "could not" sleep due to physical issues (caffeine, racing heart, racing mind, too much sugar (let's be honest, he ate nothing that night, only unleavened bread))…But rather he did not sleep because he knew what was to come. He knew that soon, very soon death will be at his doorstep.

In the loss of my child. In the loss of Conor's father Dave. When R.L. Dobson and Mary Ann passed away from this world. In each of these, the physical separation at death occurred. This same grief will overcome over us.

Remember, *That is ok*.

Grief is ordained. Jesus grieved.

Grief is an honorable. Jesus honored Lazarus' family in tears when he wept.

Grief is ever expansive. The deeper we loved, the deeper grief will be. We are still grieving Jesus today.

And Grief is ever changing. It is your experience and one that is unique to you.

There may also be times where the body is healed but the mind continues to grieve. Or vice versa.

David in Psalms questions grief in this way. He actually speaks to himself, to his own soul in the following verse.

> *"Why are you cast down, O my soul, and why are you in turmoil within me?*
> *Hope in God; for I shall again praise him, my salvation and my God."*
> *Psalm 43:5 ESV*

David was asking his own soul *why are you downcast?*

David was a man of faith, a man after God's own heart. And yet his soul was downcast. He was even questioning why his soul should be downcast in light of his faith.

But David knew that the body and soul are separate beings. The body and soul will experience pain differently, and heal in different ways, over different timelines.

In Psalm 43:5, David was experiencing pain in his soul even though his body was praising God - and he wondered why his body would feel better and his soul would still hurt.

We too may feel this.

Our body may feel better. We may be attending church on Sundays, volunteering at local ministries and returning to life as normal – but our soul may still be in incredible pain. This is God's way of showing evidence of things unseen – that there are two beings in one that make up our earthly experience.

There is a body and there is a soul. The different ways we heal from grief shows the difference between body and soul.

It is meant to show the reality of our souls and the finite length of our earthly bodies. Our bodies here on earth will die. When we do die, grief will be experienced by those who love us. But our souls will live forever!

This is why our *Grief* is ordained to be permeated with *Hope* of the Gospel. We know that we too will die. And we will be grieved upon separation from this body.

But we too will be raised in *Hope*! Just as Jesus had faith, so too we have faith and trust that this experience is temporary and points ahead to a time of reunion in Jesus Christ.

This does not ease the pain of today. The pain is still there. But it provides hope within the pain.

So let's remember…

It's ok to Grieve.

But, It's not ok to lose Hope.

Grieve today in honor of those lost. Remember that your grief will expand in direct correlation to the depth of your love. Remember that your body and soul will grieve differently, and they will heal in different times and in different seasons.

Grieving is a natural part of life, something that occurs when the body separates from the soul at death.

Honor your loved one with deep, heartfelt grief. But don't forget our destination as believers in Jesus Christ - and permeate that Grief with Hope in eyes of our future Heavenly Joy.

> *Brothers and sisters, we do not want you to be uninformed about those who sleep in death, so that you do not grieve like the rest of mankind, who have no hope. For we believe that Jesus died and rose again, and so we believe that God will bring with Jesus those who have fallen asleep in him. And so we will be with the Lord forever. Therefore encourage one another with these words.*
>
> 1 Thessalonians 4: 13-14, 17-18 NIV

CHAPTER 2

It's ok to Stop.

It's _not_ ok to Quit.

"Call a timeout!"

Shana was 32 years old when she was diagnosed with breast cancer. The mother of four children, she asked why this had occurred to her? Her fourth child, a little boy, John had just been born. After successfully working through the pregnancy, supporting her family along with her faithful husband Matthew, she was so proud to have welcomed their first little boy to their family. Neither Matthew or Shana wanted to know the sex of the baby prior to birth, so it was with great joy that Matthew learned that he had a son, a little boy.

The months after the pregnancy had all the normal adjustments of a growing family. Moving bedrooms to make room for the new little boy. All the girls now "had to" sleep in the same room…which always made for an eventful bedtime. The occasional sleepless nights came and went. But these veteran parents were hitting stride by the time little John was six months old.

Shana also took great pride in breast feeding her children. Each one she had diligently breast fed to well beyond six months of age, pumping during the day and taking every opportunity when they were together to cherish the skin to skin contact only a newborn and a mother can truly share.

Months went by with only the typical complications…a clogged milk duct here, a viral cold there and a little too much doll play for Dad with his new little boy.

The clogged milk duct seemed to come and go with a little more regularity this pregnancy. Shana brushed it off as a symptom of it being their fourth child and the fact that their little girls were bringing home a healthy assortment of new germs to their home to share with their new little brother and mother.

Probably all part of the journey, she thought. And what a joy-filled journey it was.

As nine months approached and their baby boy John was fully adjusting to solid foods, Shana decided it was time to wean their little boy, probably to be their last child and switch to all bottle feeding the last few months of this year long journey. It had been their routine with the first three children but this time it was a little more surreal.

Could this really be the last child for us, both Shana and Matthew asked?

Laying aside those questions, Shana pushed forward with weaning baby John and within weeks her milk was drying up. But those frustrating clogged milk ducts appeared to remain. As her breasts became less full, it became apparent that her left breast had a noticeable lump, on the upper part of her breast.

Assuming it was an infection or latent clogged milk duct, she called her OBGYN and asked for her advice. She recommended scheduling a visit to have it checked out, *"just to make sure everything was ok."*

A couple days later Shana was at the doctor's office and the lump had not gone away. Her breasts continued to decline and her mind had begun to wander as to why a milk duct would be so stubborn in receding. Upon examination by her OBGYN, it was recommend that they perform an ultrasound of the site to determine it's size and exact location. Shana immediately complied and within minutes the further examination had begun.

The results from the ultrasound indicated a ping pong ball size mass inside her left breast. Her OBGYN recommended seeing a specialist and getting a needle biopsy of the site. All of this seemed to be moving very quickly for a young, 32 year old mother.

But the next day, Shana was again at the doctor with a needle biopsy under way. The procedure lasted about 30 minutes and she learned that results would be back within a couple days.

She and her husband Matthew, who had joined her for this visit to the doctor, talked on the way home about what was occurring in their lives. Being strong in their Christian faith, they felt a call to stop in at their church and ask for prayer from the pastor and staff there. To pray for good news, strength to endure whatever the news may be and for their four children, Alexis, Mia, Naomi and John.

To Shana's surprise, her cell phone rang while she was at the office the next morning, and it was her doctor's office. The doctor asked if she could take time to see her that afternoon.

Shana's heart sank to the floor.

She called Matthew and while choking back tears, they agreed to meet within the hour at their church, which was only minutes from the doctor's office.

The news they received at the doctor's office was what they expected, but not what they wanted.

Shana had breast cancer.

A referral was immediately made and the next day they were at a cancer hospital in the city. Test after test brought more bad news. A further ultrasound found additional suspicious lymph nodes. A mammogram showed a suspicious pea sized mass in her right breast. It was all just too much to handle.

Words like mastectomy, lumpectomy, hysterectomy, E-something positive, P-something negative, gene mutations and genetic testing were all packed into a seven hour marathon meeting with doctors.

And there was that nasty word Chemotherapy mentioned because some reception thing was positive.

It was all just too much. They were given several options to consider and the doctors asked if they would let them know the next day what path they'd like to take.

Tears were no longer part of this game. Shana and Matthew were well beyond tears. Shock, frustration, anger and denial were all whirling around in this tornado of life.

> *Could this really be me? Shana asked.*
>
> *We've been so faithful, to each other and raising a family, why us? Matthew inquired.*
>
> *What in the world was going on? And we need to make a decision by tomorrow? Aghhhh!!*

How were they going to make a decision by tomorrow?

For those of you who have faced a moment like this in your life, you know what Shana and Matthew are feeling.

You've gone from being a perfect *"American Dream family"* carving your pathway through life…to an *"I'm staring down the grim reaper"* the next week.

Only a matter of days changes perspective and the break-neck pace of life quickly turns into a snail's pace as whole lifetimes are experienced each day. Life slows to the point it is painful to wait and patience is a premium.

Your body tells you to accelerate to find a solution. Your heart aches as you feel hurt by the every appointment. And your mind is mush as words you never thought or spoke are thrown at you in bunches.

This is the moment to call a ***TIMEOUT!!!!***

Timeouts are used in sports when the opposing team has made a big run, when the offense is sputtering, the play clock is running low and when the players are tired.

In life, we can do the same thing. We can call a timeout. We can ask for a few minutes, a day or even a few weeks to pause, collect our thoughts, get a second opinion, have a discussion with your pastor, your spouse, your parents or just go to a room so you can scream at the top of your lungs!

Shana needed some time, so she took it. She paused, and called a timeout.

She called the doctor and said, I'm going to take a few days to think about the decision.

Michael was a middle-aged actor. His diagnosis of early onset Parkinson's was not only a shock to him, but also to his fans around the world.

Michael J. Fox had starred in the *Back to the Future* series early in his career and several hit comedies in the years that followed. He recounted the early years of his diagnosis for an interview with The Guardian:

> *After he was diagnosed with Parkinson's disease, but before he started writing books about optimism, Michael J Fox went <u>through a period of seeing himself as he thought others saw him</u>.*

"Peculiar," he says, was the overall impression. "Funny looking.

[Parkinson's] makes me squirm and it makes my pants ride up so my socks are showing and my shoes fall off and I can't get the food up to my mouth when I want to."

Mr. Fox had been a movie star for five years when he was diagnosed, and was used to being stared at. But of course this was different.

"I hate the way it makes me look," he thought. "That means that I hate me."
(Emma Brock, The Guardian, April 10, 2009)

Michael wrestled for years with acceptance of what lay ahead of him after his diagnosis. He struggled with how he was going to look and how others would look at him.

He was used to being stared at but not for "shaking uncontrollably."

He was not ready to accept that he would be subject to such a disease. He was so uncomfortable with it, he did not disclose it for many years.

It took him from 1991 when the initial diagnosis was made until 1998 to finally disclose his early onset Parkinson's to the public. His reaction to his illness is a typical first response - denial, confusion and anger.

In the midst of Michael's struggle he made a choice to stop - to call a timeout - to pause for a few years and continue his life without the "burdens" of the diagnosis and the "stare" he would get.

Michael's timeout was a long one. It lasted for nearly eight years before he accepted the gaudy stares and revealed his diagnosis.

Michael's timeout was unlike Shana and Matthew. His timeout was eight years long.

In Shana's case, she did not have that long. She had cancer and did not have years or even months to decide. But she did have days and weeks. So she too called a timeout. She stopped and said…

> "I will not make a decision tomorrow. I will call you when I am ready to talk. My family needs me here. I need to pray about this. I need to clear my head. My husband needs to marshal resources for the journey. My mother

needs to fly in from Boston, MA and I need a *timeout*. I will call you when I'm ready to call you."

A week later, she was ready and made her decision about a path forward. Double mastectomy, recovery and then a full course of chemotherapy.

Number of Timeouts?

In the game of life, our timeouts are limitless. We are not governed by some referee watching for penalties and fouls. We are governed by a God that is one in three persons, who himself called a timeout often - Luke speaks of these times in his Gospel.

> *"Yet the news about him spread all the more, so that crowds of people came to hear him and to be healed of their sicknesses. <u>But Jesus often withdrew to lonely places and prayed.</u>"*
> Luke 5:15-16 NIV

And in the midst of the most trying time, Jesus stopped again, calling a timeout to muster the strength to venture on.

> *"He withdrew about a stone's throw beyond them, knelt down and prayed, 'Father, if you are willing, take this cup from me; yet not my will, but yours be done.'"*
>
> Luke 22:41-42 NIV

A timeout for us can be called when it's time for you to make a big decision. A timeout can be called to accept what you've just been told, news of a death, diagnosis or tragedy. A timeout can be used in the middle of a major appointment, at the bedside just before surgery or at home at the dinner table. A timeout is simply a call to **STOP!**

To stop for a minute, an hour, a day or even a few months or years - because you need time to process what's ahead of you.

In calling a timeout, we acknowledge that when life accelerates to a pace to which you cannot adjust you need to tap the brakes and slow down. Sometimes it's a light tap on them, just to take a deep breath or get a fresh cup of coffee. Other times, it's a full fledged slam on the brakes, throwing life to a screeching halt. Sometimes you have to walk out of the appointment and say, "*I'll call you next week...*"

Remember this -

When Life is not ok…

It's ok to call a timeout.

How to use timeouts?

Jesus shows us a great example of how to use timeouts judiciously. He never stopped pursuing his destiny, that of a cross and redeeming death. But as we see in the gospel narratives, Jesus also paused often to take a moment and process the magnitude of the moment. Whether at the tomb of Lazarus, the pursuit of crowds or at the most difficult moment in his mission on earth, his impending death - in each case Jesus withdrew, sometimes just to weep and sometimes for a lengthy, weeks-long fast.

Whatever the case, the key to using timeouts is acknowledging they are only stopping points on the journey.

Timeouts are not the end of the journey.

Timeouts are used to pause the tape and breathe in the moment.

If we don't pause at these moments, our ability to process emotions, gather information and sort through results will be overwhelmed. Just as Jesus used timeouts, so we too can use them to pause and allow time for our body, mind and soul to catch up with our circumstances.

My Personal Timeout Story

Having lived through two cancer diagnosis' and the death of our son, I've had this experience first hand.

Life was accelerating so quickly it was tearing us apart. I was going one direction and my wife in another, while the doctor was driving a wedge deeper into our marriage - make the decision now, Chemo or not? Start Tuesday or not?

Timeout!!!

On several occasions my wife and I agreed to use a timeout. Our longest timeout was a three week pause, from December 9th to after Christmas in 2013, choosing to wait to start Chemotherapy for my cancer until after the celebration of Christ's birth had passed.

Christmas has been my favorite season of the year for my entire lifetime. We had young children, ages 2, 5 and 7 at the time, who equally loved the miracle of Christmas. We acknowledged that had I started treatment, our Christmas would be consumed by IV's, pain medications and puking.

So by God's grace, we mustered the strength to ask the doctors,

> *"Is their any risk to waiting three weeks to start chemo, pushing back our start date from the 9th of December to after Christmas?"*

The answer was no, there was no risk in waiting...and probably a lot of wisdom in letting my body heal from three surgeries, three surgical infections and allowing the marital wedge to heal, if only for a few weeks.

So we called a timeout, celebrated Christmas with no noticeable health burdens and took on the first days of Chemotherapy while welcoming a new year on December 31st.

It was the best timeout I've ever called.

Using a timeout for a period of time is healthy. When a diagnosis comes, acceptance of it's impact on your life and denial that it's actually occurring happen at the exact same time.

It's like a beef vegetable soup, you love the meat but have to deal with the vegetables in it.

Shana loved her life prior to cancer, but now cancer is part of her life soup, and it's now something she has to eat. She has to make a decision how to move forward, but that decision does not have to be right now.

You may face the same scenario.

A tough decision may need to be made, but it does not have to be made right now.

Timeouts and Eternity

I want to stress a few things about timeouts.

First…timeouts are not quitting.

And saying I quit, is not a timeout.

Remember that.

Calling a timeout does not mean you've quit.

As a matter of fact, in major college and professional sports timeouts are used to help <u>win</u> the game!

When the game is going the wrong way and the opposing team is in the middle of a 10 to 2 run, the coach calls a TIMEOUT!

The team has not quit, they just need to regroup, get a drink of water, a word of encouragement and an adjustment to the game-plan - and then march back on the court to finish the game. When you call a timeout, remember that you're not quitting, you just need a moment to regroup.

The second lesson:

> *Second...those closest to you may not like how you use your timeouts.*

When you call a timeout, your doctor, a family member or a close friend may not like the fact that you need a timeout. There may be pressure to make a decision now, move forward tomorrow and start treatment next week. That pressure is ok and so is your decision to say no, I need a timeout. If they don't like how you use your timeouts, that's ok, because they are your timeouts - not theirs.

Just as an opposing coach does not like when you call a timeout in the middle of their 10 to 2 run, those closest to you may not like how you use your timeouts.

Remember, they are your timeouts, you decide how and when to use them. So use them the way you want.

The Third Lesson:

Third, I want to stress that timeouts near the end of our journey are not giving up.

When your journey is near its end, timeouts can be critically important. When treatment aimed at fighting the disease is no longer worth the physical and emotional cost – you call a timeout on treatment and let the disease run its course.

This timeout may feel like you or your loved one is quitting. It may feel like *giving up* - and that can be very demoralizing, upsetting and frustrating.

You want to fight on, you want them to fight on.

But calling a timeout on treatment, whether life threatening surgery or a drug that will nearly kill you, is not giving up.

I have a friend who's mother had cancer. His mother had treatment options that were very harsh and would nearly kill her if taken...but rather than take the treatment, she decided to embrace rather than run from her last days on earth. She called a timeout, adjourned the family of four boys and told everyone she was offering her suffering for everyone's eternity.

Calling this kind of timeout is acknowledging that the end of our journey in life is but a birth into a new eternal journey. There are times when you and the other people in your life will not agree on timeouts that are called. This is not the outcome for which either of you hoped. Taking a permanent timeout from treatment, remember it is only a timeout, not quitting, in the eyes of God.

Sometimes illnesses will come steal the mind like a thief in the night. Alzheimers does this. And sometimes like in cancer, ALS or Parkinsons disease, the body is affected but the mind remains full of zeal.

In each case, there may come a time when a permanent timeout on treatment may be needed so as to not damage the soul.

What God cares most about is your eternal soul. If you need to embrace what is happening to your mind and body calling a timeout in order to preserve your soul, God is right with you.

If you call a timeout on treatment to your body or mind in order to save the soul, you've not given up, but embraced eternity ahead.

And last, and this is most a most important lesson...

Quitting only occurs when we give up on God.

I think timeouts are a God-given gift to our free will. God gave us the ability and the right to stop. To stop when life is too much. When the pace has accelerated. When the news is all bad, and treatments can only make it worse. While our minds and bodies deteriorate in this life, I believe our soul only matures and grows wider and deeper as we age to embrace the trials of our lives.

In this journey, we may call many, many timeouts. God only asks us one thing - to never give up on Him and what he did on the cross of Jesus Christ.

These are the words of our Triune God, Father, his son Jesus Christ and their Holy Spirit.

> *"Remember that I have commanded you to be determined and confident! Do not be afraid or discouraged, for I, the Lord your God, am with you wherever you go.""*
> Joshua 1:9 GNT

> *"Come to me, all you who are weary and burdened, and I will give you rest. Take my yoke upon you and*

learn from me, for I am gentle and humble in heart, and you will find rest for your souls."
Matthew 11:28-29 NIV

"But do not forget this one thing, dear friends: With the Lord a day is like a thousand years, and a thousand years are like a day. The Lord is not slow in keeping his promise, as some understand slowness. Instead he is patient with you, not wanting anyone to perish, but everyone to come to repentance."
2 Peter 3:8-9 NIV

The Lord has his purpose in all things. But his purposes do not focus on our mind or body. Rather, they focus on our soul.

Jesus most especially stresses this in Matthew 11:28-29, pleading with us to call a timeout, come to Him and find rest for your soul.

Remember, it's ok to call a timeout.

Stop, turn to the Lord and say, *ok Lord, I'm with you now in the quiet, dark night of the soul, on the day before you suffered and died. Please pray with me for the strength you had to give up your body and mind, in order to save my soul.*

It's ok to Stop.

It's ok to call Timeouts.

You have an unlimited number of timeouts. Call them as often as needed.

Just don't ever Quit.

Never quit on God.

"Jesus went up on a mountainside and called to him those he wanted, and they came to him."
Mark 3:13 NIV

"When evening came, Jesus and his disciples went out of the city."
Mark 11:19 NIV

"They went to a place called Gethsemane, and Jesus said to his disciples, "Sit here while I pray.""
Mark 14:32 NIV

"Then Jesus went up on a mountainside and sat down with his disciples."
John 6:3 NIV

CHAPTER 3

It's ok to relish the Sunrise.

It's not ok to hide from the Sunset.

This was one of the most difficult circumstances. You have a young woman with a brand-new baby. Of course, everybody is fighting for every chance that she's got. She was young. She's enthusiastic. She wants to tackle this. You don't want to be the downer. So you're looking, you're grasping for a straw that says, "Well, there's something here that's going to be beneficial."

Stage 4 lung cancer...we know it's not curable, but suppose she's the one that somehow gets cured. Maybe she's the one. And so therefore, we should do all these things to her.

Having any kind of discussion that would begin to say, "Look, you probably only have a few months to live. What do we do to make the best of that time, without giving up on the options that you have?" That was a conversation I wasn't ready to have. I don't think any of us were.
~ Dr. Atul Gawande, from Being Mortal ~

Peering at the sunset of life comes to us all. I do not have a profession that permits me to stare into the end of life on a daily basis.

Dr. Atul Gawande does.

Dr. Gawande is a surgeon, writer, and public health researcher. He practices general and endocrine medicine at Brigham and Women's Hospital in Boston, Massachusetts.

In his personal reflection, he discovered that it was difficult to communicate the end of life with his patients. Imagine the situation…a young mother, a new baby, Stage IV lung cancer and death at the doorstep.

How would you communicate?

I had a friend who died early in his life. He was 19 years old.

I distinctly remember finding out that it happened. Our college life was interrupted by the news…*seriously, he was dead?*

We all dropped everything…and rushed to the family's hometown. It was a town small enough that you could drive through it and blink, almost missing the church where the funeral was held.

But that tiny Catholic Church the day of the funeral was packed full. The Pastor's eulogy sunk deep in me and I've never forgotten his words. He said,

> *"I minister to people.*
>
> *I perform weddings, baptisms, participate in ordinations. But the favorite part of my mission journey on earth is to minister to the sick and dying.*
>
> *Ministering in this world, this culture today, in all other phases is so temporary.*
>
> *Men and Women marry - and they divorce.*
>
> *Children are born into broken homes.*

Ordination has become a status symbol and not a call to serve.

It's all been perverted.

But we cannot pervert and cheat death. We can only embrace the circumstances. And knowing Robert for his whole life, he knew in the eternal grace of the Lord Jesus Christ, he would be accepted into his heavenly home."

I was stunned. Totally stunned by those words.

Who in their right mind would find joy in this?

Death had always been uncomfortable for me. For Dr. Gawande, it was uncomfortable because his job was to find a cure. For me, it was the discomfort of death because I was young and death was seemingly far away. I was totally perplexed how someone could actually find joy in this moment.

Dr. Gawande found the sunset of life just as difficult to manage as I did. In his documentary film, "Being Mortal," he reflects…

Being mortal is about the struggle to cope with the constraints of our biology, with the limits set by genes

> *and cells and flesh and bone. Medical science has given us remarkable power to push against these limits, and the potential value of this power was a central reason I became a doctor.* <u>*But again and again, I have seen the damage we in medicine do when we fail to acknowledge that such power is finite and always will be.*</u>

Hope for a cure is something doctors stake their careers upon. Doctors have pushed the limits of death. It is the central reason Dr. Gawande chose his career.

We cannot and must not spend our days focused on death. We must relish the sunrises of our lives.

We must relish the puppy love of dating, the first kiss and marriage or vocation as it is revealed to us.

We must love our faith and it's journey through baptism and rebirth in this life.

We must stop and soak in the birth of a new baby son or daughter. Staring into the miracle of life.

We must live in the present moment of life.

But, in relishing the sunrises, we cannot forget that at every moment, at every turn there is someone else in this world near their sunset. That death is forever linked to life until the return of Jesus Christ.

While Dr. Gawande is not a follower of Jesus Christ, his view on life and death is valuable as he faces it every day. And he acknowledges they are missing something. He further shares…

> *We've been wrong about what our job is in medicine.*
>
> *We think our job is to ensure health and survival. But really it is larger than that. It is to enable well-being.*
>
> *And well-being is about the reasons one wishes to be alive. Those reasons matter not just at the end of life, or when debility comes, but all along the way. Whenever serious sickness or injury strikes and your body or mind breaks down, the vital questions are the same: What is your understanding of the situation and its potential outcomes? What are your fears and what are your hopes? What are the trade-offs you are willing to make and not willing to make? And what is the course of action that best serves this understanding?…*

Doctors are not called to be the minister of death. They do not come sharing a message of no hope. They love sunrises as much as we all do. The cure, the longer life and return to health!

I had the same experience in my cancer diagnosis. I was told I had Melanoma in my lymph nodes.

An extremely dangerous cancer had spread. And we did not know what lay ahead. My doctor laid out the realistic circumstances, honestly and openly. He shared his view of the situation, that life and hope were real and relevant.

But he also shared that death was a realistic outcome, with a relatively high chance of occurring. That could perhaps be near it's end. That we may be staring into my sunset.

Dr. Gawande struggled with this kind of conversation. Sharing further he stated…

> *I've been a surgeon for more than a decade now. In medicine, your first fear as a doctor is that you're supposed to be able to fix a problem, and our anxieties include wanting to seem competent, and to us, competent means I can fix this…*
>
> <u>*Among the most uncomfortable difficulties was grappling with those cases where we couldn't solve the problem. The two big unfixables are aging and dying.*</u> *You know, they're not— you can't fix those.*
>
> *How is dying ever at all acceptable? How is it ever anything except this awful, terrible thing? And the only way it is is because we as human beings live for something bigger than ourselves.*

Dr. Gawande understands it.

Fr. Richard Rohr explains it.

Near the end of life, the veil becomes 'very thin.'
Fr. Richard Rohr

Fr. Richard Rohr, is the founder of The Center for Action and Contemplation. He has spent his career calling men and women to the present, to the here and now. Live life to the fullest.

As death is part of life, he has spoken numerous occasions on the topic of death. And he speaks of it with great joy.

Fr. Rohr has stated being close to the dying is a great benefit to his life. His ministry as a priest brings him there frequently.

As he ministers to the dying, he has found that the veil between heaven and earth becomes very thin. Events of life near death reveal the eternal glory literally just moments away from the dying person.

His view of death is integrally linked to scripture. In the Old Testament, the Lord instructed his people to place the Ark of the Covenant behind this veil. The Ark was contained in the temple, behind a holy veil was the Holy of Holies.

> *You shall make a veil woven of violet, purple, and scarlet yarn, and of fine linen twined, with cherubim embroidered on it. It is to be hung on four gold-plated columns of acacia wood, which shall have gold hooks and shall rest on four silver pedestals. Hang the veil from clasps. The ark of the covenant you shall bring inside, behind this veil which divides the holy place from the holy of holies. Set the cover on the ark of the covenant in the holy of holies.*
> Exodus 26 32-24 NABRE

This veil was torn, literally torn down the center, and heaven ripped open on Calvary's hill when Jesus died.

> *But Jesus cried out again in a loud voice, and gave up his spirit. And behold, <u>the veil of the sanctuary was torn in two from top to bottom.</u>*
> Matthew 27: 50-51 NABRE

Fr. Rohr has experienced that the veil between life and death is no longer a physical separation between earth and holy of holies as in the Old Testament. Rather, at the cross, Jesus tore this veil and opened heaven. For those bound to

Jesus in this life, the veil becomes very thin near death, and you can see into the heavenly destination of life.

It is a beautiful view on life and death.

The cadence of life will bring death to us all.

Dying is like that summer sunset on the day you never want to end. That summer sunset happens every day. It may happen quickly, with the sun disappearing below the horizon before you have a chance to even see it. Or it may be that you watch that sunset, incrementally, slowly descending across the horizon seeing every light disappear and every night-time star appear over in the darkening night sky.

> Beautiful sunrise. Beautiful sunset.

> Beautiful life. Beautiful death.

John is a friend who's father passed away after a long life. Well into his nineties, driving to and fro nearly to his last day on earth. John's father was a an amazing lover and caretaker.

John knew the days were drawing near to a close. He knew that the sunrise was approaching. He spent time with his parents. He visited often and loved his parents. Spending time staring into those sunrises of life.

Memories of basketball games and weddings.

Memories of discipline for stupid choices.

Memories of children and grandchildren born.

Memories of ice cream on the back porch.

His mother passed away in the winter that year. His father so loved her, he died shortly after in the spring.

My father did not live as long as John's. Only into his seventies. I did not get the chance to stare deeply into the sunrises of my life with my father. But that does not mean we did not relish the sunrises.

At his funeral, we shared story after story of our father. He was a man of many faults. He sinned like we all do. But his faith shines through and our mother is a beautiful women to have loved, endured and chosen life with my father. She was married to him for 54 years, with ten children born and over 40 grandchildren & great-grandchildren.

A beautiful life my father had.

A beautiful death my father endured.

To achieve his glorious crown of new life.

There is no sunset without a sunrise.

There is no death without life.

Don't take this message as one to live in fear of death. Or in anticipation of death.

Please don't stop relishing in those sunrises of life. Rather, relish in them more every day.

Love your husband.

Kiss your wife.

Hold your grandchildren.

Visit and just sit with your parents.

Light 55 candles on your double nickel birthday and nearly burn down the house.

Jump around with your kids as they dance the night away to Disney music.

Break all the rules. Eat ice cream for breakfast. Cookies for lunch. And smores for dinner…

It's ok to love and live and move and breath…

It's ok to relish the Sunrise.

What is not ok?

To hide from the sunset.

It is coming.

With every sunrise, a new sunset is being prepared for our fulfillment and joy. At each sunrise the un-fixables of life, as Dr. Gwande calls them, *Aging* and *Dying*, are set into motion.

A life that will be lived out a day at a time. With opportunities for love, life and hope. Many, many sunrises to come.

But if you are near or someone you know is near that sunset on life, sit with them and relish in those sunrises. Stare into the sunset of that life. It is full of colors, emotion and an incredible end of an incredible day.

In each sunset on life, the beauty and grandeur of the minutes of those persons life emblazoned the sky the day of that celebration.

Yes, I feel the same way as Dr. Gwande asking those same questions.

> *How is dying ever at all acceptable? How is it ever anything except this awful, terrible thing?*

Why me? Why now? Why us? Why so quickly? Why not more time?

I lost my son to death after only 90 minutes. I ask those questions. I certainly ran back to the damn sunset and yelled at God. I was upset, grief-filled and weary.

But trust in the Lord.

Don't focus on the lost sunrises of life. Stare into the sunset. Open the veil to heaven. Sit and trust as Fr. Richard Rohr does, that this veil is torn and very thin.

Stare into the sunset and watch as the colors change, hues are mixed and as the night time star scattered sky appears. It is beautiful this design God has for our life.

Faith, Hope and Love.

Turn to Life Eternal.

It's ok to relish the Sunrise.

It's not ok to hide from the Sunset.

Don't let the sunset consume your life. Love every sunrise. And cherish, relish and stare into the sunset as it comes to an end.

It is permanent as the pastor over my friends funeral shared.

It is life.
It is death.

It is permanent in this world.
It is eternal in Christ.

> *Christ is glorified in me when people see Jesus is more precious to me than all that life can give or death can take.*
> Rev. John Piper

The sun rises daily on our lives here.

Relish in every sunrise.

But our sunset nears every day here on earth. Death shall come.

Don't hide from the Sunset.

Embrace the colors of this eternal life transition and let it guide your path every day.

But tell me this—since we preach that Christ rose from the dead, why are some of you saying there will be no resurrection of the dead? For if there is no resurrection of the dead, then Christ has not been raised either. And if Christ has not been raised, then all our preaching is useless, and your faith is useless. And we apostles would all be lying about God—for we have said that God raised Christ from the grave. But that can't be true if there is no resurrection of the dead. And if there is no resurrection of the dead, then Christ has not been raised. And if Christ has not been raised, then your faith is useless and you are still guilty of your sins.

In that case, all who have died believing in Christ are lost! And if our hope in Christ is only for this life, we are more to be pitied than anyone in the world.

But in fact, Christ has been raised from the dead. He is the first of a great harvest of all who have died.

So you see, just as death came into the world through a man, now the resurrection from the dead has begun through another man. Just as everyone dies because we all belong to Adam, everyone who belongs to Christ will be given new life. But there is an order to this resurrection: Christ was raised as the first of the harvest; then all who belong to Christ will be raised when he comes back.

After that the end will come, when he will turn the Kingdom over to God the Father, having destroyed every ruler and authority and power. For Christ must reign until he humbles all his enemies beneath his feet. And the last enemy to be destroyed is death.
1 Corinthians 15: 12-26 NLT

"Where, Death, is your victory?

Where, Death, is your power to hurt?"

Death gets its power to hurt from sin, and sin gets its power from the Law. But thanks be to God who gives us the victory through our Lord Jesus Christ!
1 Corinthians 15: 55-57 GNT

When I saw him, I fell down at his feet like a dead man. He placed his right hand on me and said, "Don't be afraid! I am the first and the last. I am the living one! I was dead, but now I am alive forever and ever. I have authority over death and the world of the dead."
Revelation 1: 17-18 GNT

CHAPTER 4

It's ok to be Angry.
It's _not_ ok to be Bitter.

This deadly cancer of anger from which so much harm grows: It makes us unlike ourselves, makes us like timber wolves or furies from Hell, drives us forth headlong upon the points of swords, makes us blindly run forth after other men's destruction as we hasten toward our own ruin.
~ St. Thomas More ~

Holding a grudge is like swallowing poison expecting someone else will die.

I remember speaking with a close friend, Barb, after her spouse had passed away. She met her husband in her late teens and married in her early twenties. Over 40 years of marriage, Barb was loved deeply, but as in any relationship of depth and length, she was also hurt many times.

Her husband did not respect her as a mother - he golfed too much early in life leaving it to her to raise the young children. One of their children had been left handicap after nearly suffocating during birth. Barb's own mother had committed suicide a few years into her marriage ripping life's anchor from the ocean floor setting her adrift for many years.

Barb and her husband had been blessed with many children and grandchildren. And a few of them had wandered off the straight and narrow path, bringing much stress into her life.

And due to the financial burdens of a large family, her retirement nest egg was smaller than that of her friends. So with her husband's death, Barb was now tied down to a fixed income while her friends spoke of travels to beaches, foreign lands and famous sites around the world.

As I spoke to her, I learned of her past, present and future. She was still young, in her 60s. The spirit of her life began to pour out of her like old, seasoned bourbon. Sweet, yet with strong odor and lasting taste.

Her life was one she cherished but her spirit felt as if she had been tarnished by the circumstances of her life. It was like the joy deep within was hemmed in by events, experiences and emotions that stained her sweet spirit.

I pressed in and asked her if she was ever mad. Did she feel angry at some of the circumstances of life? The stress of young children, the lack of support early in life, the tragic suicide of her mother, her child's handicap and the grandchildren gone astray…

Somewhat perplexed by the question, Barb said, "Yes."

I asked if she was ever angry at someone in her life. Her husband, her kids, her mother… Pausing, she stared out the window and said, "Yes."

I then asked her if she was ever angry at God. For not being there. For leaving her lonely. For the handicap child. For the loss of her mother. For letting wave after wave overcome her.

Even more perplexed she stared off into the distance crinkling her eyebrows as she thought… and after several seconds of silence while in that car together, Barb again said, "Yes."

My final question was simple.

I asked her if she had ever told God she was angry at Him. Had she ever spoken out loud to God that she was angry about her mother's suicide, her husband's lack of respect or her children's bad choices.

Barb did not respond. She stared blankly out the windshield as the white dashed lines raced under our- car - as meter after meter of road went by.

She raised her hand to her face and rubbed her eyes. This clearly hit a nerve as the weight of the question caused tears to flow down her face.

C.S. Lewis, a British novelist and lay theologian, writes of anger in his book, *"A Grief Observed."* The book chronicles his feelings after his wife Joy died from cancer only a few short years into their marriage.

After penning such books as *"Mere Christianity"* which both became a theological Christian necessity, Lewis was now tormented by questions about faith. He had gone from being a man of great faith, to one who was simply angry with

God. He wrote with honesty and truth regarding his desperation and painful doubts.

He concluded that his faith in God was a *"house of cards"* that collapsed in one fatal blow - the death of Joy, his wife.

In *"A Grief Observed,"* he gave himself permission to rail against God and to be consumed with anger. He wrote:

> *Meanwhile, where is God? When you are happy...so happy that you have no sense of needing Him...so happy that you are tempted to feel His claims upon you as interruption, if you remember yourself and turn to Him in gratitude and praise, you will be—or so it feels—welcomed with open arms.*
>
> *But go to Him when your need is desperate...and what do you find? A door slammed in your face...after that, silence...The longer you wait, the more emphatic the silence becomes...*
>
> *Why is He so present a commander in our time of prosperity and so very absent a help in time of trouble?*
>
> *...Not that I am (I think) in much danger of ceasing to believe in God. The real danger is of coming to believe such dreadful things about Him. The conclusion I dread is not, "So there's no God after all," but, "So this is what God is really like. Deceive yourself no longer."*

Lewis' anger with God arose because he lost the love of his life. Having met in their 50's, Lewis and Joy quickly fell in love and married. He had waited over 50 years to find Joy. He loved her deeply writing to one friend soon after their marriage,

> *"It's funny having at 59 the sort of happiness most men have in their twenties ... Thou hast kept the good wine till now."*

Within months of this writing, she was sick, dying only a few years later.

Lewis loved her so that when sickness bore it's weight on her body, his anger with God grew.

I can relate to Lewis.

I remember the day I was diagnosed with my second form of cancer in less than three months. I was standing in my bedroom with my wife, staring blankly at the wall. I was about to explode. In my mind's eye, I was picturing putting my fist through the sheetrock wall.

I was fuming with anger. Anger at cancer. Anger at sickness. Anger at the surgeons. Anger was rippling through my veins.

The only thing that stopped me from assailing the sheetrock was the ravaging side effects of multiple surgeries and a series of infections - I had so little strength left, I could barely stand.

By this time, my emotional state was in tatters. In 2013, the same year of my cancer diagnosis, our family had been assaulted by disaster. Before my cancer diagnosis in September, our son James had died in June of a rare birth defect. This was now December, and a second primary cancer diagnoses pushed me over the cliff of anger.

Anger opened in me like an oil gusher from deep inside coating my entire body. I literally could feel it in my toes, rising rapidly consuming my entire body.

In the three years prior to that moment, I had been on an intentional journey to lead and foster a family of faith, hope and love. Through this work I had spent many hours with God reading his word, leading bible studies and developing a love relationship with Him.

I had written a book, started a Christian blog and studied scripture extensively. My wife and I had been on retreats, we loved our children, served our Lord...

Much like Lewis, I felt betrayed. Angry at God.

I thought...now this was my reward? Cancer!?!?

I regularly railed against God.

Yelling at him for not letting me sleep in the middle of the night. Closing my eyes, silently screaming at God as the needle was inserted in my arm for the next treatment...and the next treatment...and the next treatment...Kicking and screaming inside as my children watched my body tremble and quake at the side effects of treatment.

Reading the words of C.S. Lewis in a "Grief Unveiled," they so rang true.

Why is He so present a commander in our time of prosperity and so very absent a help in time of trouble?

...Not that I am (I think) in much danger of ceasing to believe in God. The real danger is of coming to believe such dreadful things about Him. The conclusion I dread is not, "So there's no God after all," but, "So this is what God is really like. Deceive yourself no longer."

I was hurting so bad and God was not showing up. He simply was not there.

The pain was not just physical. My eldest daughter had started a chemo chart for me in my bathroom - just like her potty training chart from years before where I rewarded her for each successful potty - she returned the celebration, now placing a sticker for each successful chemo treatment. For each self administered chemo needle inserted, I received one sticker.

This little shift from father teaching daughter to daughter helping father was so painful. She was only seven years old...and she had to watch this happen to her father.

Through it all, I was so angry at God. *Where had he gone?* I felt like Lewis...thinking I was not about to cease believing in God, but rather believing such terrible things about Him.

I was not about to give up on Him. I trusted Him. I had built a relationship with Him. He was my only solution. I continued to reach out even in my anger.

Numerous times I turned Christian music on so loud I could hear nothing other than the words of worship reverberating against the walls of my bedroom. I tried to drown out the pain, if only for minutes at a time.

Nothing worked. The pain remained.

And through it all, God pursued me.

I've discovered since then to be angry at God is not a sin. To be angry at God is not wrong. God pursued me through my anger. And I believe God pursued C.S. Lewis even as he railed against God when his love passed away too young and grief overwhelmed him.

In hindsight, it was so good to be angry at God. So good to have that raw emotion.

But how can this anger be good?

Since those days I've learned so much about anger. The core is that anger is a positive emotional response. Anger is not an original emotion. It is a response emotion.

Anger occurs in response to love.

Jonathan Parnell writes for Desiring God ministries and in an article titled "*What our anger is telling us?*" He shares this:

> *Traditionally, the anger issue has been divided up between those who get angry and those who don't. Some personalities tend toward red-faced eruptions; others are unflappably relaxed and easy-going. But the truth is, everyone gets angry — it's just expressed in different ways. And why we get angry has to do with love.*
>
> *In one degree or another, anger is our response to whatever endangers something we love. "In its uncorrupted origin," says Tim Keller, "anger is actually a form of love."*
>
> *<u>Anger is love in motion</u> to deal with a threat to someone or something we truly care about. And in many ways anger is a right response.*
>
> *It is right that we get angry with the delivery guy who speeds down our street when our kids are playing in the front yard. That makes sense. The delivery guy puts our children in danger.*

Anger is not only ok.

Anger is love in motion.

Everyone get's angry. That is if they *love*.

Parnell is correct in his assessment. It is right to be angry at someone who has stolen from your home, your family. It is right to be angry when death takes your spouse or child. It is right to be angry when you are diagnosed with cancer.

It was right for Barb to be angry. Her husband had died. Her life had been difficult. Her next steps were so uncertain.

It was right for Lewis to be angry. At 50, he finally found his love. And now, she was dead.

It was right for me to be angry. At 31, my son was dead. And cancer treatments had ravaged my body.

Scripture accounts for the fact that we will get angry, just as God became angry.

God was angry at the Israelites dozens of times in the Old Testament through repeated cycles of covenant and betrayal.

> *Behold, the name of the Lord comes from afar, burning with <u>anger</u>, and his burden is heavy; his lips are full of indignation, and his tongue like a devouring fire; his breath is like an overflowing stream, which reaches up to the neck, to sift the nations with the sieve of futility.*
> Isaiah 30: 27-28 ESV

> *And the Lord said to Moses, 'I have seen this people, and indeed it is a stiffnecked people! Now therefore, let*

> *me alone, that my <u>wrath</u> may burn hot against them'*
> Exodus 32: 9-10 ESV

God also expresses his anger out of love. He loves his covenant people. He wants them to keep the covenant so as to sustain life giving fruit.

His love for the chosen Israelite community extended into anger toward those who endanger his chosen tribe.

> *I will execute great vengeance on them with furious rebukes; then they shall know that I am the Lord, when I lay my <u>vengeance</u> upon them.*
> Ezekiel 25:17 ESV

Accept that anger is ok. Accept that it is a love emotion. Accept that love and anger are forever tied together. We will only 'be angry' at something that endangers someone we love.

Approaching anger from this angle allows us to frame "anger," rather than just try to avoid it.

Let's be honest…just saying, *It's ok to be angry* gives us a release.

Say it again…

It's ok to be angry.

It's good to be angry.

It's good to love.

But here is where the rubber meets the road.

We cannot stay angry forever.

In the New Testament, Paul teaches the people of Ephesus on anger in Ephesians 4:26. Paul shares,

> *"Be angry and do not sin;*
>
> *do not let the sun go down on your anger, and give no opportunity to the devil."*
> Ephesians 4:26 ESV

The start of this verse is a quote from David's Psalm 4:4.

> *"Be angry and do not sin."*
> Psalm 4:4 ESV

David endorsed anger. "Be angry," he says. It's weird to read that.

"Be angry."

That is so counter cultural. To say I'm just going to "Be angry." We now say, "Be happy!"

But what we've learned is it's ok to be angry. It's ok to be angry out of love.

But David buckles this teaching to a second teaching. Let's not miss this. If you are angry, you are also to not sin.

Paul builds upon this point, specifically teaching the Ephesian people to *not let the sun go down on your anger, and give no opportunity to the devil.*

There is a correlation here. Both David and Paul are teaching us when consumed with anger to have a guard for attacks from devil and vulnerability to sin.

But what happens if we never leave the state of anger? What happens if we stay angry?

As I reflected on my conversation with my widowed friend, I saw that she was angry. But something had happened to her.

Her sweet spirit had been put out by a cone of bitterness.

It was ok for her to be angry. But we cannot stay there. Something failed to happen with her anger and rather than releasing it, anger had stained her sweet soul, covering it in a thick coating of tar.

It had made her bitter.

David and Paul write to direct us to do something with anger. Being angry for long periods of time, or to put it another way, harboring anger, creates vulnerable, access point where sin, shame, fear, and guilt can penetrate repeatedly ravaging the soul.

The point is not whether or not we will become angry. It is about what we do with that anger. In the second part of Ephesians 4:26 he states…

> *Do not let the sun go down on your anger, and give no opportunity to the devil.*

This is a very stern warning about anger.

Paul is very direct. He knows how vulnerable we are in a state of anger. He tells we cannot carry anger with us even unto the next day. He is extremely direct.

> *"Do not let the sun go down on your anger."*

This confused me when I first read this teaching. If in fact "Anger is a Love Emotion," then what becomes of love?

If we love, then what happens with our resulting anger?

If anger has it's origins in love, then what happens when I love more?

The truth of the matter is that…

> ***The more we LOVE, the more we will experience ANGER.***

The correlation is simple math. The more people we truly, deeply love, the more we will be angry we will be when those people are hurt, damaged or die.

So should we simply love less? Should we lock out doors, unplug the phone, drop social media and cease all friendships?

Foolish! This is *foolish!* Paul would say!

Paul is not telling us to love-less in order to avoid anger. He is telling us to learn how to deal with the anger emotion.

We will be angry. Even angry with God at times.

But we must not let anger overwhelm and consume us.

We must not let the sunset on our love.

We must not let the sunset on our anger.

When C.S. Lewis was overcome with grief he did not dismiss the anger emotion. Rather he ran toward it.

When I was on chemotherapy, I did not run from the pain. I allowed others to suffer the pain with me. Even my own seven year old daughter.

Barb on the other hand had suppressed the anger. Not let it come out, but rather held it in.

Lewis and Barb had the same experience of anger, but a different end result. Barb had her soul stained by the years of suppressed emotion. This stain manifested itself as bitterness.

Read this short parable and follow the path of the two men, looking for the difference between the burdened and those set free.

> *One day, two monks were walking through the countryside. They were on their way to another village to help bring in the crops. As they walked, they spied an old woman sitting at the edge of a river. She was upset because there was no bridge, and she could not get across on her own. The first monk kindly offered, "We will carry you across if you would like."*
>
> *"Thank you!" she said gratefully, accepting their help. So the two men joined hands, lifted her between them*

and carried her across the river. When they got to the other side, they set her down, and she went on her way.

After they had walked another mile or so, the second monk began to complain. "Look at my clothes," he said. "They are filthy from carrying that woman across the river. And my back still hurts from lifting her. I can feel it getting stiff." The first monk just smiled and nodded his head.

A few more miles up the road, the second monk griped again, "My back is hurting me so badly, and it is all because we had to carry that silly woman across the river! I cannot go any farther because of the pain."

The first monk looked down at his partner, now lying on the ground, moaning. "Have you wondered why I am not complaining?" he asked.

Then the first monk knelt down beside his companion, placed his hand on his back and said, "Your back hurts because you are still carrying the woman. But I set her down five miles ago..."

There it is!

Both of those monks carried the same burden - the old woman by the stream. But one monks experience resulted with a deeper sense of joy - *he smiled and just nodded his head* - while the second monk ended with a deeper sense of bitterness.

So bitter that it incapacitated his physical, emotional, intellectual and spiritual well being.

Barb & C.S. Lewis were both angry too. Both suffered the loss of a spouse. Both had burdens of life.

Lewis and Barb had been wet with tears just as the monk was wet with river water. Lewis was burdened with the physical hardship of being a widow, just as Barb was. Lewis had a deep anger emotion just as Barb had.

But Lewis' result was different. He did not end his life a crippled and angry man as the burdened monk had.

Rather, Lewis ended his life as a joyful, prayerful man. His last book was not one of bitterness and fear. Rather he finished his works with the book *"Letters to Malcolm: Chiefly on Prayer"* passing away before it was published. Lewis was writing about the joy of prayer to God late in his life. He was faithful to the end.

Barb on the hand had been so burdened by the unreleased anger that it crippled her Spirit. She had not set down her anger and was now laying on the ground unable to speak or move forward.

I too shared the anger Lewis harbored. Death, sickness & hardship had shipwrecked our life and I was stranded on the shore of a desert.

I was angry.

But I am not an angry man today.

I was daily *alive* in those moments of anger! I was present to my anger. I was not unconscious to the pain in this life and in this world. Rather, I lived it. I don't think we are called to avoid anger. Avoiding anger does not make it just go away.

Having been through the anger experience in this way, I now have a deeper perception of pain. I am more centered and aware of hurt. I've been moved from sympathy to empathy for others in their weakness.

But how?

I started this journey by first saying it is ok to be angry.

Say it with me now…*It is ok to be angry.*

Freeing isn't it.

Say it again…*It is ok to be angry.*

Deep breath's now…say it again.

It is ok to be angry.

Now the journey can begin. Accept the anger, pick it up and carry it across the river with me now.

In my experience, the turning point happened when I was ok being angry. I was so pissed off and I was ok with it.

As the weeks passed, I began to notice a change. The correlation between love and anger began to become apparent.

I was not angry at my cancer.

I simply loved my wife and my children.

I was not angry at our doctors who did not have a medical solution for our son James who died.

I simply loved him.

I began to write about it. I observed my anger trying to understand its origin. As I'd lay in bed at night, shaking with a fever waiting for the pain medication to dampen chemo's side effects, anger would gush forth again. I'd observe it and realize I was not angry at the medicine or the cancer…I was angry because my wife and children had to see me this way.

And I loved them.

Not until years later did I hear the words…

> *"Anger is a Love emotion.*
>
> *Anger is Love <u>in</u> motion."*

Just as Grief is an honorable feeling for a lost loved one, anger too is a natural emotion that should not be buried.

Anger is not wrong.

Anger itself is not a sin.

Think of this fact. Jesus became angry. And He was sinless.

Therefore, anger cannot be a sin.

Observe Jesus in Mark's Gospel.

> *And he looked around at them with <u>anger</u>, grieved at their hardness of heart…"*
> Mark 3:5 ESV

Anger is ok.

However, when anger is not released as Paul teaches us, it will be perverted and will infect your being.

When anger is held for years and years it will consume us.

When anger is not released, the doors will open to spiritual attacks. The physical affects of which can be *eternally* harmful.

When my son passed away, I was angry at God, at me, at the doctors, at everyone. When I was diagnosed with cancer, it compounded exponentially the emotional response. All consumed by anger. All consumed.

I loved my son. He was gone. I was angry. That was ok. I loved my family and my life was now at risk.

But something deep inside welled up. A spirit inside would not quit. It was ignited by the love of Christ. And his trust in me. And my trust in Him.

I realized I could not stay there.

Jesus knows we will become angry because he too became angry. In fact, I think he wants us to be angry. Because anger is love in motion.

But we cannot stay there. If we do, the anger will turn on us. It will fester like an infection slowly spreading into resentment, rage, disgust and envy. If anger is not released and transformed, the cycle will consume us. Just as the second monk could not release the woman from his back and anger harbored in his body for several miles crippled his physical being, so too our anger will cripple us.

When anger turns to *bitterness* it cripples us.

I believe we all know a few *bitter* people. Think of them for a moment.

Those who are bitter at a spouse that left.

Perhaps bitter at a drunk driver who killed their child.

Or bitter at a disease that marred their life.

It could be that they are bitter at God who seemingly has not heard their pounding at His door!

Stop for a moment and observe. Recognize that in each and every case, bitterness is not an original event. It is not an event at all.

Recognize that bitterness is not an original emotion. It is not an emotion at all.

Bitterness is rather the after effect of anger consuming your life, infecting your being and overcoming your spirit made in the image of God. Bitterness is the hangover of anger that you just can't shake.

Bitterness occurs when anger consumes our being. Anger changes you. It turns you from the person you were, into a bitter person.

So you are angry. Or someone you know is angry. Or you are bitter. How do I change this? How do I get up from this crippling burden of bitterness?

Don't worry. We are not isolated on the journey. C.S. Lewis felt the same. He discovered that regardless of what he tried, he continued to struggle with anger and despair over the loss of his wife. He wrote that…

> *"It doesn't really matter whether you grip the arms of the dentist's chair or let your hands lie in your lap... The drill drills on."*

Anger and despair are not one time shots. It reoccurs throughout life, surfacing and then fading again only to resurface as another loved one is inevitably hurt.

As Lewis said, the *drill will drill on*...Regardless of whether we grip the sides of the chair or not.

But there is hope. If you feel stuck, that's ok. Just tell yourself you will not stay stuck forever.

If you feel you can't move on. That's ok. Just tell yourself you will be able to move at some point.

Tell yourself, I won't stay in this place.

But how?

The tool given to us by Jesus is *Forgiveness*.

Forgiveness is a divine tool for releasing anger. But it is also incredibly difficult.

C.S. Lewis writes of forgiveness in his book titled "The Weight of Glory."

> <u>You must make every effort to kill every taste of resentment in your own heart</u>—every wish to humiliate or hurt him or to pay him out. The

difference between this situation and the one in such you are asking God's forgiveness is this. In our own case we accept excuses too easily; in other people's we do not accept them easily enough...

...Even if he is absolutely fully to blame we still have to forgive him; and even if ninety-nine percent of his apparent guilt can be explained away by really good excuses, the problem of forgiveness begins with the one percent guilt which is left over. To excuse what can really produce good excuses is not Christian character; it is only fairness.

<u>*To be a Christian means to forgive the inexcusable, because God has forgiven the inexcusable in you.*</u>

This is hard. It is perhaps not so hard to forgive a single great injury. But to forgive the incessant provocations of daily life—to keep on forgiving the bossy mother-in-law, the bullying husband, the nagging wife, the selfish daughter, the deceitful son—how can we do it? Only, I think, by remembering where we stand, by meaning our words when we say in our prayers each night 'forgive our trespasses as we forgive those that trespass against us.' We are offered forgiveness on no other terms. To refuse it is to refuse God's mercy for ourselves. There is no hint of exceptions and God means what He says.

So you've been hurt and you're angry. Forgive.

So it's been fifteen years and you're bitter. Forgive.

It's been a lifetime since the childhood you regret. Forgive.

It's been another day, another week or another year of pain. Forgive.

Who has wronged you? Who has hurt you? Who has hurt the one you love?

Forgive.

God means it when He says unforgiveness is a hell-bent sin. The Bible says that if you do not forgive those who sin against you, God will not forgive you (Matthew 6:15).

In other words, this is an immortal issue. An ongoing, unforgiving, bitter, and angry spirit will kill a person's heart, shipwreck their faith and prove that they never belonged to God in the first place. God is showing you how serious this sin is.

That's what Paul instructs us to…

> *"Forgive one another, as God in Christ forgave you."*
> Ephesians 4:32 ESV

"Be kind to one another, tenderhearted, forgiving one another, as God in Christ forgave you."
Ephesians 4:32 ESV

Forgiveness is one of the hardest things to do in life. Especially when the person is 100% guilty!

But read C.S. Lewis again. The greatest tool in forgiveness is to acknowledge your place. Acknowledge how much you have been forgiven by God through Jesus and it will create a spirit able to forgive others the same.

Remember that God will vindicate your just cause and settle all accounts better than you could. Give it to Him.

Either your offender will pay in hell, or Christ has paid for him. If you do not release it, the payback would be double jeopardy or an offense to the cross. The cross is enough.

Let go and forgive the offense.

Let's remember that if we love, we will face Anger. Anger is ok. It is a love emotion divinely rooted.

However, bitterness is not ok. It is a place, that defines your immortal spirit. It defines you as a person. Don't be a bitter man or woman.

Don't stay angry. Don't carry it with you as the monk did. Don't let it define you. Ponder how much you have been forgiven and return the forgiveness to the one that has harmed you.

It's ok to be Angry.

It's not ok to be Bitter.

Forgive and find love again.

"Therefore each of you must put off falsehood and speak truthfully to your neighbor, for we are all members of one body. "In your anger do not sin": Do not let the sun go down while you are still angry, and do not give the devil a foothold.

Get rid of all bitterness, rage and anger, brawling and slander, along with every form of malice. Be kind and compassionate to one another, forgiving each other, just as in Christ God forgave you."
Ephesians 4:25-27, 31-32 NIV

CHAPTER 5

It's ok to HAVE Fear.
It's *not* ok to BE Afraid.

Peace I leave with you; my peace I give you. I do not give to you as the world gives. Do not let your hearts be troubled and do not be afraid.

~ John 14:27 NIV ~

It's 2 a.m. on the Navy destroyer USS Trayer, and the air is thick with the smell of fuel and 350 crewmen who have been working too many hours. It's another long, monotonous shift of routine maintenance when, suddenly, the night is ripped open by the piercing wail of an emergency alarm.

The Trayer is under attack. Explosions rock the ship as fires burn and the anguished cries of the injured fill the air. To escape the flames, the flooding, and the thick smoke, the men and women of the crew scramble through mangled compartments past gruesomely torn bodies. Lights flicker, turbines whine, metal rips, and the relentless scream of the alarm tells everyone what they already know: This is war.

Except it's not.

As the recruits battle flame and rising waters and treat the wounded, Naval petty officers stand by, observing and evaluating the performance. The officers can remain almost eerily unflustered amid the chaos because the attack, and the ship itself, are simulated.

Dubbed the unluckiest ship in the Navy, the USS Trayer is under siege nearly every day at its mooring in a 90,000-gallon tank inside a cavernous building at the Recruit Training Command in Illinois. This long night of fire and flood—the exercise lasts 12 hours and runs through 17 different scenarios—is the elaborate and exhausting culmination of eight weeks of training. Every year, 37,000 recruits are subjected to the high-tech terror of the Trayer.

"This is supposed to feel real," says Michael Belanger, PhD, a Navy senior psychologist, who headed the team that designed the $60 million landlocked ship. "This is supposed to scare the recruits."

Mission accomplished. After his night in hell, Seaman Recruit Colt Bailey emerges from the Trayer weary and streaked with soot. "We were all scared and stressed out," says Bailey, who boarded the Trayer for training last summer and panicked when he had to step into smoke so thick, he couldn't see. But the 20-year-old from Eagle, Idaho, fought through his fear and kept going. Weeks of study—how to fight fire, how to move the wounded—had left him more prepared than he knew. "I learned I can trust my training," he says. "I know there will be other times when it's real, when it goes a step further, and I'll be scared. In that moment, I hope I do what I did on the Trayer."

The military counts on it. Each branch uses high-tech simulations: Battlemind (now called

Resilience Training) is an Army and Marine Corps exercise in which troops inside a Humvee experience an IED attack and firefight.

Fear should be our best friend. It's a chemical reaction, a signal to pay attention to a threat. It's our brain alerting us to danger, triggering the classic fight-or-flight response—sweaty palms, dry mouth, an increase in breathing and heart rate & a jolt of adrenalin—to help us survive. But when the brain doesn't return to normal after a stressful incident, or when there are too many incidents, this hormone-driven alert system can turn toxic.

"You don't want someone without a fear response at all," Mujica-Parodi says. "That's not brave; that's just abnormal. But a high stress response is also unhealthy." The optimal fear response, she says, accurately assesses risk, saves room for cognitive thought, and rapidly returns to baseline when the danger passes. *(Source: "How the Science of Fear Makes Soldiers Stronger" Kathryn Wallace, Reader's Digest 2015)*

The Fear Response

The military has tried for years to manage the fear response. Preparing young soldiers using assets such as the Trayer has become the norm. This management of the fear response has been going on for centuries. General George S. Patton is often quoted as one of the best military leaders of the 20th century. He led men into battle during World War II and is credited with leading the final charge into Germany to end the war. The general is well known for his quotes during times of difficulties and one in particular regarding fear.

> *The time to take counsel of your fears is before you make an important battle decision. That's the time to listen to every fear you can imagine! When you have collected all the facts and fears and made your decision, turn off all your fears and go ahead!*

General Patton was not a fearless man. Rather, he was a man full of fear. He acknowledged the fear response and his goal was to manage that response. A soldier's fear is the same fear that we all face as an instinctive response to a dangerous situation. As the Readers Digest article stated, *"Fear should be our best friend. It's a chemical reaction, a signal to pay attention to a threat."*

Fear in Medicine

Hospitals have taken this approach as well to address patients in time of great stress. Dana-Farber Cancer Hospital in Boston, Massachusetts has many publications on the topic of fear. Their research around cancer and fear has determined that the most distinct fear of a cancer survivor is the *fear of recurrence*.

Once you've been through the initial treatment and survived the initial fear of having cancer, the fear of recurrence can become overwhelming. It's emotional, psychological and physical toll can consume your life like a tidal wave, similar to that of the sufferings of a war veteran struggling with Post Traumatic Stress Disorder (PTSD).

The hospital has posted several videos of survivors who have to deal with this fear.

One in particular from a woman named Julie, who is a Melanoma cancer survivor, chronicles the initial diagnosis on her right leg followed by a recurrence on the same leg six years after initial treatment. She lives with daily fear that Melanoma could reappear and once again flip her world upside down.

Julie's fear is the same fear that I deal with daily. Having had two forms of cancer at 32 years old, I am grateful for the healing hands of doctors that cured me and pray for a long life well into my retirement years. But I am continually filled with the fear of recurrence. The fear is unavoidable.

Before cancer, I was a healthy, thirty two year old former Division I college athlete. I was <u>not</u> going to die until old age came.

But death, like a gypsy, came to steal what I loved.

The gypsy appeared in the form of cancer.

I wrote this on caring bridge (a blog we kept to keep our family and friends informed of the status of the disease and treatment) in the weeks after the diagnosis.

> *The Truth is this. I have written with conviction in the past and in this present time about faith...but the Truth is I am incredibly full of fear and doubt. I am struggling to find that mustard seed size faith inside me right now.*

I was awash in the fear of the diagnosis and did not know which way to turn.

Fear does not just consume soldiers in battle and cancer patients - it impacts all aspects of our lives. Harvard Business Review offers a view of fear from a business perspective in an interview with Peter Gruber, former chairman of Sony Entertainment. Mr. Gruber is quoted.

> *"Fear can paralyze or catalyze an organization. A leaders' willingness to embrace fear dictates how successful they and their enterprise may be."*

Fear can be a cause of paralysis in business, great loss on the battlefield in war, and consume our lives in the fight for life in a cancer patient.

My fear of cancer caused paralysis in the fall of 2013. The fear in my life was apparent. I had a singular focus on the fear of mortality. I would die leaving my wife and children behind to fend for themselves. Fear was consuming me.

Having fear vs. Being Afraid

I have counseled with many cancer patients in the years that have followed my own diagnosis. In those conversations, I have discovered there is a difference between having fear and being afraid.

Having fear is a natural, instinctual response to a situation that endangers our well-being - whether it comes from an external source as in a battlefield situation or an internal source such as cancer growing inside you.

On the other hand, <u>being afraid</u> happens when we allow that fear to consume our daily activities.

To be or not to be? That is question.

It is not asking whether we should have fear. The questions is, *<u>to be</u> afraid or not <u>to be</u> afraid?*

When an external or internal fear becomes who we are and how we define our lives, we have gone from *<u>having fear</u>* to *<u>being afraid.</u>*

President Franklin D. Roosevelt, the 32nd President of the United States, is often quoted as saying...

"The only thing we have to fear is fear itself."

He also quoted as saying, *"Men are not prisoners fate, but prisoners of their own minds."*

Fear is a universal emotion, driven out from deep within our souls, as a survival instinct. We've all gotten a real or irrational jolt of fear from the sight of a hairy spider or a slithering snake. As a basic survival mechanism, fear helps to keep us safe from danger. We react with a "fight or flight" response — tensing our muscles, freezing in place preparing for a fight or instantaneously running for the hills.

Peter Gruber experienced fear in business when his company was threatened. Julie experienced fear when her cancer reoccurred. And the military prepares recruits to manage this fear in basic training, knowing fear will occur.

Fear rises from deep within as a survival instinct.

It quickens the heart rate.

Tenses the muscles.

And piques our eye sight and hearing.

Fear is a God-given tool used to survive the most difficult circumstances. However, when fear goes from becoming an instant reaction to a constant drumbeat of anxiety, worry and tension, we have succumb to the survival instinct and permitted fear to become who we are.

We have _become afraid_.

In the days before the results of my lymph node surgery, I had abandoned myself to despair. I was in a completely frozen state of mind. All I could think about was the results. I no longer had fear…rather I was afraid of what I was going to find out.

When I entered the doctor's office, I was overcome with emotions and concerns for what I was about to find out. The day that I found out I had a second form of cancer, I posted this on my Caring Bridge site…

> *So, we take the good with the bad. Good news…No more Melanoma in the lymph nodes. Bad news…I have Thyroid Cancer. This is not a perfect world. Hell, let's be honest, Jesus was born a cute, cuddly baby, wrapped in swaddling clothes only to die on a damn cross a few short years later. Many of you have battled cancer as well or know someone who has, and*

it's not pretty, it's not noble or mighty. It is work. A work which I will undertake with Joy.

On that day, fear changed in me. I had so much thrown at me, going from one diagnosis to two, that I had only two choices...to let the despair overwhelm me or begin to find a way out.

On that day for the first time, by the grace of God, fear was transformed into a brief moment of joy. For a brief moment, I was no longer afraid of what was to come. Rather, I had a first glimpse of the pathway from fear to faith.

In embracing what was to lie ahead for a purpose greater than myself, I had for the first time unbuckled my fear from being afraid. My being was no longer defined by fear.

This change happened only in brief moments at first. After I wrote that blog post, I had several more moments where fear overwhelmed me - for example, being afraid of chemotherapy. Afraid of the end of life. Afraid of leaving a widowed wife. Afraid of the needles. Afraid of the medical bills. Afraid of everything.

But at each occurrence, I always recalled the first day I had overcome my fear. The day I had chosen to fight against becoming afraid with the grace and power of God.

Jesus Christ spoke often about being afraid. He compared having peace to being afraid in John 14:27 saying…

> *"Peace I leave with you; my peace I give to you. Not as the world gives do I give to you. Let not your hearts be troubled, neither let them be afraid."*
> John 14:27 NIV

Jesus contrasted the everlasting peace he left with us to the troubled, afraid hearts we often have. He did not leave us with this statement without also leaving a roadmap to our way out.

In the verse following John 14:27, in John 14:28 Jesus says…

> *"The Advocate, the holy Spirit that the Father will send in my name—he will teach you everything and remind you of all that told you."*
> John 14: 28 NABRE

Jesus promises that we will not be left to our own circumstances without the help of the Holy Spirit. Jesus says to acknowledge our mortal bodies and the fears that come with that mortal being. But rely upon the Helper, the Holy Spirit to walk you through those times of distress.

Dana-Farber Cancer Institute acknowledges says the same thing. They give two specific tools to deal with fear.

> **Acknowledge the fear** - Accept that you sometimes may worry about cancer coming back.
>
> **Talk about it**. Don't fall to the tyranny of silence. It's OK to talk about your fears and concerns, either for yourself or for a loved one. Communicate what everyone is feeling.

I recognize daily that a recurrence of my cancer could occur. But I do not live in fear of it reoccurring.

Rather, I have a group of men and women I talk to regularly about fear, running from the tyranny of silence to the power of the Holy Spirit at my most fear-filled moments. With those men and women, I break the tyranny of silence in my heart with an outward groaning praying for uncommon peace despite the circumstances of the day.

And when fear becomes too much for even my own soul to handle and it distracts my daily activities, I remember one simple verse from Romans chapter 8, verse 26:

> *Likewise the Spirit helps us in our weakness. For we do not know what to pray for as we ought, but the*

> *Spirit himself intercedes for us with groanings too deep for words.*
> *Romans 8:26 ESV*

My goal in life is no longer to avoid fear. I know it is a God-given survival instinct, an emotional response to a situation in my life that could cause injury or pain. I don't try to avoid fear.

Rather, I trust my fear, knowing it is trying to protect me and then I pray that the fear that wells up within will drive me deeper into faith that the Holy Spirit by his *'groaning too deep for words'* will pray me through the fear to greater faith.

Don't belittle, look down or criticize yourself for having fears. It is part of our human nature. Don't take those fears and harbor them within the tyranny of silence, allowing them to grow roots in your soul. Rather, use those fears to hone your focus on Christ, the ultimate Joy at the end of life.

Saint Pope John Paul II stated,

"Do not abandon yourselves to despair. We are the Easter people and hallelujah is our song."

Remember, it is ok to have Fear.

It is not ok to be Afraid.

"Do you give the horse its strength or clothe its neck with a flowing mane? Do you make it leap like a locust, striking terror with its proud snorting? It paws fiercely, rejoicing in its strength, and charges into the fray. It laughs at fear, afraid of nothing; it does not shy away from the sword. The quiver rattles against its side, along with the flashing spear and lance. In frenzied excitement it eats up the ground; it cannot stand still when the trumpet sounds. At the blast of the trumpet it snorts, 'Aha!' It catches the scent of battle from afar, the shout of commanders and the battle cry."
Job 39:19-25 NIV

"Keep your lives free from the love of money and be content with what you have, because God has said, "Never will I leave you; never will I forsake you." So we say with confidence, "The Lord is my helper; I will not be afraid. What can mere mortals do to me?""
Hebrews 13:5-6 NIV

ABOUT THE AUTHOR

Through this journey of life, Benjamin Hartings has buried a son, beaten cancer two times, married an incredible wife, raised four beautiful children, written three books and read exponentially more. Benjamin is the youngest of 10 children, a faithful husband and a devoted father. He coaches soccer, watches football, loves to read and shoot clays. His golf game could use some work and his roots are tied deeply to the work ethic and discipline he learned growing up on a small poultry farm in Ohio.

Most of all, he is in love with his wife, Lynn. He cherishes his children, four of whom are here on earth - Grace Mary, Thomas Lester, Katie Lynn and Daniel Benjamin - and one of whom is up in heaven – his son James Thomas.

But before he reads or writes anything, Benjamin first tries to spend time every day with his savior Jesus Christ. He prays for you to find peace and joy in Him as you read and reflect on this book and that of his other writing.

BENJAMIN J. HARTINGS

Other book by the Author:

RETURN TO THE ALTAR
A Sacred Journey Through Grief & Joy

The story of Ben & Lynn Hartings life, birth and death of their son, James Thomas Hartings.

Published:
December 4, 2014

---

www.Intersect-Me.org
Ben's blog can be found
at this website.

Contact: BenHartings@gmail.com

The Lord is at hand; do not be anxious about anything, but in everything by prayer and supplication with thanksgiving let your requests be made known to God. And the peace of God, which surpasses all understanding, will guard your hearts and your minds in Christ Jesus.
Philippians 4: 6-7 NIV

www.ingramcontent.com/pod-product-compliance
Lightning Source LLC
Chambersburg PA
CBHW022111090426
42743CB00008B/804